Published by Sheryl Spanier and Karen Otazo

ISBN 144141407X

www.sherylspanier.com

www.global-leadership-network.com

www.notime4theories.com

Author portraits: Ian Spanier
Editor: Nick Kolakowski
Graphic Designer: Mike Bain

The Portable Executive

High-End Career Management

BY SHERYL SPANIER AND KAREN OTAZO

Contents

PICTURE THIS...

You're chatting with other senior executives at a holiday party. The conversation focuses on successes of the year and plans for the future—until the topic of the disabled economy comes up. Suddenly, everyone in the room seems to be sharing their fears for the future of business, reflections on and comparisons of historical downturns, and professional horror stories.

One colleague, the burned-out CFO of medium-sized advertising firm, voices his current dilemma. In his 30 years in the business, he's never seen things so slow. There's little to do, no growth plans and the firm has downsized as much as it can without closing. With all that in mind, he's fantasizing about taking the winter off to operate a ski lift for a season—then returning in April renewed and able to figure out what's next for him. He says that he can stay in touch with the office remotely and fly back if anything comes up.

What would you say to him?

YOUR DECLARATION
OF INDEPENDENCE

Every day and everywhere, you are inundated with a changed and changing marketplace. Our corporations, governments, economies and education systems are being transformed. While traditional models will certainly survive and thrive, new opportunities have grown for you to expand and adapt your mindset about career management for yourself and your organization.

In our first guide, *Leave Happy*, we termed this constantly shifting environment the "Post-Millennium Workplace." Within this new paradigm, the speed of information transmission has made the global workplace more fluid—and capable of changing in milliseconds. Along with a flatter, faster and virtual workplace, there has emerged a more ambiguous and non-linear career management imperative.

If you are a leader who is:
- Wondering what's next
- Examining the meaning of your work
- Seeking more career control
- Assessing your future options
- Leading a worried, wounded or weary team

Then this guide is for you.

Career Portability Replaces Career Path

For years, individual success—defined as personal job security, longevity and loyalty—was the currency that supported stable, growing organizations. However, this idea has started to become outmoded. In its place is an atmosphere of anticipation and anxiety in which fearful leaders and teams hunker down, fight to keep what they have intact or flee their organization in pursuit of other opportunities. Job security pressure strangles organizations right when they need to be nimble, innovative and in a "constant change" mode.

This seismic shift represents an opportunity to re-define how careers are made and managed, in keeping with the emerging "flat," innovative and rapidly changing companies of the future.

Work continuity will replace job security. Look at each "variable" in the formula below—are you truly portable? If not, what can you change?

Portfolio Of Valuable Achievements (EXPERIENCE)
+ Solid And Sustained Relationships (EXPOSURE)
+ Understanding Of Marketplace Needs and Trends
(EXPERTISE)= Portability

You can no longer expect to maintain job stability and security. Instead, ask yourself how to make your work "continuous" by offering competitive value.

Work continuity is supported by:
- Experience
- Expertise
- Exposure

And made possible by its commercial value:

- Needed (fills a professional, personal, business, societal deficit)
- Wanted (speaks to a marketplace demand)
- Monetized (is worth a financial investment for the buyer and can support you)
- Viable (pragmatic, strategic, lasting or expansive)
- Supported (attracts "buyers," stakeholders, followership)
- Known (visible to, and valued by, potential customers)

Reset your expectations. Build your portability rather than succumb to being a one-company, one-industry, one-function leader. Freedom derives from a self-managed career plan that replaces an organizational career path. Portable Executives are able to dedicate their time and talents to their current commitments and create value. Their achievements build a portfolio that supports their internal and external Portability.

In this new environment, ask yourself:

- How will you adapt?
- How will you keep your team focused and functioning?
- How will your workers flourish?

YOUR PATH TO PORTABILITY

Take a few minutes to figure out how to broaden the image of your career road map beyond your title, scale, prestige, territory, power, and compensation:

- What are you? (Example: Marketing Leader Expert in Emerging Markets)
- What can you do? (Connect with global money-making sources and opportunities that may not be obvious)
- Who needs what you offer? (Consumer product companies, startups, venture capitalists, media)
- Who will pay? (Companies, entities, investors, government)

AVOID THE FOUR 'F'S
Guard against the common limbo-state impulses of Freeze, Fear, Fight and Flail.

Redefine Your Career Identity

"When one door closes, another opens. But we often look so regretfully upon the closed door that we don't see the one that has opened for us."
— HELEN KELLER

Imagine you're at an industry event. You find yourself next to a leader in your field you've been interested in getting to know. After brief niceties, he asks you the inevitable question:

"So, what do you do?"

What do you say?

Your professional career management mindset kicks in when asked this question.

Most people speak of themselves in terms of where they work—we'll refer to this as "context." In this mental model, Career Identity rests in a sense of affiliation, where the brand, prestige and reputation of your organization all define you.

Other responses to the "what do you do" question might focus on:

- Content (what you do functionally or your profession)

- Mode (how you work: employed, entrepreneur)
- Status (your title, retired, in transition, recently downsized)
- Industry (your field or profession)
- Personal (your family, generation, geographic location, circumstances)
- Retrospective (what you used to do)
- Prospective (what you want to do)
- Humor (you're still trying to figure that out!)

How you describe yourself creates an impression. What you lead with drives the rest of the conversation.

Portable Executives know one thing for sure: We are all always in transition. As a consequence, every executive is perpetually self-marketing, seeking connections, and interested in what others are doing. They are curious about ways to contribute and learn and are very conscious of how to position themselves when asked, "What do you do?"

How Did You Get Here?

The first step to becoming a Portable Executive is to review your "How Careers Happen" mindset. Cycle back through your memory and take a look at the steps that led to your seniority.

You may say:
- "I kind of fell into this field."
- "I was recruited right out of school and advanced along the way to this point."
- "I never really thought about it. It just happened."
- "It was a happy accident."
- "I guess it was a little bit of insight and a little bit of random stuff just coming along—plus a bit of trial and error—before I found work that provided purpose and meaning."
- "I really wanted to be an actor/artist/architect/ farmer, but my parents pressured me to join the family business... and here I am."
- "Luck, I guess."

Insights from your answers will provide

information about how you expect to grow, change or evolve professionally. You may find, ironically, that you never really had to think about, plan or pursue your work.

Like most successful leaders, you rarely think about your career unless it becomes threatened or disillusioned. When that happens, you may be asking:

- Is that all there is?
- Whatever happened to my dreams?
- How can I do something that has more meaning...without giving up my lifestyle?
- With all the changes in my company/industry, I find the joy gone. How do I discover what I am passionate about?
- If I am no longer a Senior Vice President at [X Company], who am I?

In some ways, these internal dialogues throw you into a kind of professional adolescence, one in which you feel adrift and unclear about your identity, but nonetheless possess a plethora of potential. You need courage, information and a system to explore, consider, pursue and have confidence in alternative choices. You may even find yourself confronted with an ultimate choice:

Do you define yourself by your work?
- Does your career identity support personal meaning and enjoyment?
- Or do you pragmatically see work as a tradeoff, where you earn a high income to support your lifestyle?

Give yourself more choices. Decouple your professional identity from your workplace affiliation.

Examine—And Eliminate—What Holds You Back
Think about your career. What comes to mind? Are you looking for security blanket–style comfort and nurturing? If driven by security, your career choices may have been dominated by responding to

imperatives:

- You go where the organization needs you.
- You build a fortress of allies and loyal staff, figure out how the politics work, and numb yourself to the constant organizational shifts.
- You count on your organization to provide career opportunities, advancement and regular raises in compensation.
- You operate with a "good student" mentality: "If I work hard and do well, my company will promote me accordingly."
- Your career identity is your organization.
- Your answer to the "What do you do?" question is usually, "I work for Company X."

Or, you might describe your work as a prison:

- You feel obligated to follow a career path within an organization or field that's not of your choosing.
- You find little intrinsic pleasure or purpose in your work and end up dragging yourself through the weeks feeling empty, unfulfilled and stuck.
- You feel trapped and your self-esteem plummets, limiting your options. Your work quality suffers.
- You are vulnerable to derailment, demotions or downsizing.

If you're in this position, "What do you do" may prompt you to answer briefly, perhaps negatively, and then want to change the subject. In some situations, you might actually complain about your career or organization, or make a flip or abrupt comment about trying to figure out what to do when you "grow up." That might earn you an empathic chuckle...before your listener starts looking over your shoulder to seek out a more interesting conversation. Power brokers are generally not interested in undefined adolescents who aren't family.

Pride in your workplace, willingness to do what it takes to make your company succeed and loyalty to your boss, mentors and sponsors are critical career success factors. There is a risk, however, in becoming overidentified with a particular company (security blanket) and/or trapped by a career (prison). Entangled, you burn psychic energy staying put. Under the belief that you have few options, you stay hunkered under your blanket or barricaded in your prison to keep safe.

This style of laying low has often protected good corporate citizens in the past. In the fast-paced and lean organizations of the future, though, those who limit their sense of adventure, enthusiasm, creativity and risk-taking may miss out on advancement in the Post-Millennium Workplace.

Make a Platform, Not a Prison

"The dreamers of the day are dangerous men, for they may act their dream with open eyes, and make it possible."

— T.E. Lawrence, also known as Lawrence of Arabia

Let's go back to the "work as prison" example.

First, it is very common for the self-sacrificing, external success–motivated, modern day executive to get trapped in a career "prison."

As a Post-Millennium executive, though, you compete in a radically different world. No longer can you expect to start your career with an employer and stay with it until you're ready to pull the parachute ripcord. Now, the workplace is one of free agency, career "upshifting," derailment, resilience and reinvention.

Successful workplace navigation requires you to see your current position as the platform for advancement or change. The work you're doing increases your worth by adding to the professional portfolio that you transport from this situation to the next. Your path can be mapped out with an understanding of what motivates you, what brings you satisfaction, and what you personally find meaningful and enjoyable.

PRISON	PLATFORM
Organization-Driven Careers	Self-Managed Career Thrust
Career Path	Career Portfolio
Builds on Past Experience	Created from Future Focus
Have Done	Will Do
Fill Available Jobs (organization chart)	Positions Created Outside the Boxes
Succession	Satisfaction
Should Do	Want to Do
Dedicated	Diversified
Protect Job	Build Future Options
Wait for Promotions	Promote Yourself

Reach out to embrace the "seismic mind shift." Recognize that bumpy, unpredictable and constant change requires personal accountability, resilience and a new way of describing yourself professionally.

Before, you may have identified yourself by the name of your current (or former) employer. Now, think of yourself as an impact player. What do you contribute? As a leader, what do you stand for?

With this in mind, your response to that "What do you do" question can become (for example), "I am a business builder," "I assure the technical foundation for business success," "I turn around and grow troubled organizations" or "I make the people side of business flourish." You're replying with your functional expertise, phrased to engage interest and dialogue.

If you're ready for some change, ask yourself the following questions:

What works for you:
- Professionally
- Personally

What works against you:
- Professionally
- Personally

How do you like to spend your time at work?
- When not working?
- What is missing?

What are some ideas you have generated regarding your next career step?
- What have you done about it?
- What gets in your way?

Outdated Mindset
While the traditional corporate relationship is now all but officially extinct, many leaders and their teams still operate on the five traditional conventional employment beliefs:

- Work is stable
- Doing everything right makes you "safe"
- Dedicate yourself to your organization
- The right position in the right organization will make you happy
- Self-promotion is not necessary in a meritocracy
- Mutual loyalty is the glue that keeps employees committed, working hard and loyal

The "Now" Mindset
- In-house workers are replaced by contractors and outsourced resources
- Entitlements and territory are replaced with strategic opportunism and partnerships
- Career Prisons open up to Career Platforms
- Self-Denial gives way to Self-Direction
- Company-dependent promotions on the organization chart morph into professional self-promotion and portfolio careers

Career Movers
Take a look at some of the following approaches to assess your habitual and historical career move methodology:
- Have you initiated change?
- What propelled you?
- When disappointed or derailed in the past, how

have you responded?

Whenever faced with obstacles, you've most likely had one of three reactions:

Attack (Go Against)
"Whoever dies with the most toys wins." (Seek retribution, rebel against an idea, person or entity—e.g., "After the company went public, I felt the new management was going in the wrong direction, so I unsuccessfully fought with the board to prove I was right.")

Check Out (Go Away)
"I will take my toys and go home" (Avoid escape; move away from or eliminate situations or people—e.g., "When I wasn't successful in driving the merger, I decided to start my own company.")

Hang On (Freeze)
"If I just keep my head down, this will all go away." (Wait out the downturns and market changes—e.g., "I will sit tight and hope that I get to keep my job.")

Have the past ways you have managed your career worked well for you?

As a Portable Executive, you can embrace another approach:

Reach for Opportunities (Go Toward)
"I have always wanted to be/have been passionate about/interested in [topic of your choice]." (Self-promote and pursue an idea, opportunity, passion, interest, people, environment—e.g., "From the time I saw the waste and lack of commitment to the energy crisis, I have focused my professional energies on building efficiency, sustainability and ethical deployment of resources.")

CAREER SATISFACTION IS AN INSIDE JOB

"Most people search high and wide for the keys to success. If they only knew, the key to their dreams lies within." — GEORGE WASHINGTON CARVER

Beware of Success Seducers

Sooner or later, many executives trade career satisfaction for career success.

You may realize that while you're considered successful, you may lack satisfaction in your work life. Many senior executives say they don't feel they have any purpose in life aside from making money; if this feeling continues, it can develop into the idea that they've "sold out" to outside influences in exchange for a title, salary and bonus. When the benefits diminish, those executives feel as if they've been left with nothing.

In your quest for career success and advancement, you may have followed a leader, accepted extra responsibility, allowed yourself to be recruited or made sacrifices. Those actions have led to accolades and accoutrements. And while that's been wonderful, you may have found yourself disconnected from an (intrinsic) sense of accomplishment.

- Have your days gotten away from you?
- Have you become estranged from what could be satisfying?
- Have you lost control of how you spend your days?

To help answer these questions, use this tool:

Part I: The Ideal Day Chart
Make a pie chart depicting your ideal workday, showing the proportion of the time you would spend on each specific activity you would choose.

Part II: The Real Day Chart

Consider how you actually spend your time. Utilize this circle to show the proportion of your day spent on each task.

Part III: The Worst Day Chart

Think about your most difficult, demanding, stressful or boring day at work—how did you spend your time?

Now compare the charts. What can you import from your Ideal Day and what would you delete from your Worst and Real Days? What stops you from converting de-motivating and limiting efforts to satisfying and career-building activities?

You can begin to create your career future one day at a time. Discover ways you can implement career transformations while in your current role. Shift just a few hours, delegate or defer draining tasks, meetings or projects and you will gain more productive time, control, impact and satisfaction immediately. As a result, you will gain energy and momentum in place of exhaustion and low morale. You will free yourself up to expand your Portable Executive attributes.

Organizations in constant flux challenge successful executives, forcing them to face change in their context or status. You may have followed a pattern of pursuing, sacrificing for and trading off for bigger and better. Now, as you consider your professional options, you have the opportunity to revisit and revitalize your career satisfaction factors.

Striking That Balance

So much executive compensation, stature and lifestyle is linked to your position; being satisfied by your work may make you hesitant to fully examine or consider alternatives, so long as you're taken care of by your successful career. As you transition into becoming a Portable Executive, though, you may consider trading these comfortable symbols of success for satisfaction.

Success is connected to context-driven external

factors, often requiring interaction, feedback and acknowledgment. When a career lacks personal energizers and engagement, the external perks start losing "Oomph."

Career identities that are dependent on success are always at risk because they require outside factors to sustain them.

Satisfaction, on the other hand, focuses on internal measures. It connects what you're doing to support your work obligations and commitments with the goal of fulfilling your personal needs, values and motivators. Determining your professional satisfaction are your personal "turn-ons" and "turn-offs."

Turn-Ons and Turn-Offs

In looking over your career, if you've discovered that your personal rise has come at the cost of trading satisfaction (what turns you on) for visible perks of success (money, power, position and politics), then it could be time to analyze and recapture what matters most to you.

Ask yourself: If you weren't taking in the big bucks, what would you be doing? What are you giving up for what you're getting? Is it worth it?

Self-Assessment Tool/Questionnaire

The mix-and-match menu on the next page allows you to assess your own career success and satisfaction themes—your career turn-ons and turn-offs, as it were.

Common Turn-ons and turn-offs at work:

TURN ONS (+)	TURN OFFS (−)
Money	Lack of funds
Corner office	Cubicle
Perks (office shower, professional and club memberships, private/company airplanes, etc.)	Lack of amenities and/or an expense account
Power	Responsibility with weak authority
Affiliation	Diminished impact or recognition
Working collaboratively	Fighting for resources
Achievement	"Losing face" in front of others
Public recognition/commendations	Lack of recognition
Industry visibility	Industry invisibility
Meeting and mixing with interesting people	Being isolated
Professional development	Threatened with downsizing or outsourcing
Mentoring	Leadership inaction
Helping others	Feeling useless
Being in the know or being informed	Missing out on information
Being sought out for opinions and ideas	Having your ideas ignored
Getting to focus on your pet project(s)	Needing to save others' projects
Completing, executing and driving results	Finding yourself stuck in bureaucracy
Creativity	Same old, same old
Launching a new initiative or project	Closing down your projects
Innovation	Following the old formula
Feeling good for doing good	Feeling like your work lacks worth
Autonomy	Dependence on others
Forecasting	Relying on the wrong historical examples
Value-driven projects	"Make-work" projects
Gains	Losses

As a Portable Executive, you can keep a realistic perspective about entitlements, implied promises and contracts. You recognize that while heroic results may earn you accolades and mega-bonuses, your past performance doesn't necessarily result in guaranteed future rewards or security.

Embrace Multiple Identities

Consider the way many creatives see their careers. As times change, they often change along with them—today's musician might not only be tomorrow's memoirist or film director, but he or she is also capable of taking up more a traditional calling, such as a carpenter, attorney or temporary worker, when need demands.

People who follow this path and embrace multiple career identities are neither secure nor imprisoned; they're continually motivated to broaden their experiences without "ego." They are, in effect, the original portfolio workers.

Prepare to be a Portable Executive via your own diverse portfolio of identities and abilities: You're a dealmaker and rainmaker, advocate and advisor to other executives, and a lobbyist.

Diversified Portable Executives find new uses for their skills and then parlay them into building the widest-ranging contact base possible. Work a little side business in addition to your main career; volunteer for assignments and projects you're passionate about; let others know that you're available in ways they don't necessarily expect. Take a page from artists' diversification techniques to anticipate your future role. Make your current occupation the platform for your future career.

Your Professional Trademark
(Demonstrate Your Expertise)

Most businesses define themselves by their brands or trademarks—consider the little ™ or ® found in the corner of an ad for high-priced liquor or a high-powered sports car. Trademark symbols, more than just a bit of legalese, officially denote the qualities of the product they represent. Clarify what makes you unique and conveys your value. You can be intentional and pithy in your professional trademark and build an association with attributes such as quality, innovation or execution strategy.

Thus, like a Ferrari or a Bell & Ross Chronograph, you too need a personal trademark—a mixture of what you do and what you pursue. As with any product or service, you will need to assess, develop, test, get feedback and constantly improve in order to stay marketable and competitive.

IPO YOURSELF: TAKING YOURSELF PUBLIC

Even the best product or service in the world is dead in the water unless it is:

- Current
- Market-ready
- On demand
- Top of mind
- Accessible
- Useful

Great brands can only stay on top with the right marketing, promotion, customer service and sales initiatives. As a smart leader, you know how to measure your organization's effectiveness in those areas. But are you applying the same metrics to your own internal and external self-marketing?

You might consider active self-promotion unseemly. If so, you likely subscribe to the following sayings:

- "Cream rises to the top."
- "Only empty suits brag about their accomplishments."
- "We work in a meritocracy. Good work and intelligence are rewarded."
- "My company will take care of me if I sacrifice and excel beyond expectations."
- "My contributions speak for themselves."

Just as great brands need to constantly advertise, promote and improve based on customer needs and satisfaction, so too do effective senior executives need to promote themselves both within and outside their organizations.

> ### *Portability Buckets* (Self-Promotion Components)
>
> - **Experience:** Range, depth, breadth and diverse qualities will trump long-term single-organization seasoning.
>
> - **Exposure:** Long-term external, professional and personal relationships combine to create a stellar reputation. Value at the top is about getting it done alongside (and through) others.
>
> - **Expertise:** At the top, it's more about what resources and strategies (based on valuable experiences) you can apply to new challenges. Getting ahead is about others choosing you as the go-to person.

As a Portable Executive, you are always marketing yourself, which actually makes you more valuable to your boss, board of directors, and stakeholders, internal colleagues and external contacts.

Keep current with all of these relationships. Build chains of mutual benefit and shared favors long before you actually need to call upon them. Control your portability. Be a valuable winner, not a vulnerable loser.

Your Professional PR

How connected and visible are you right now?

Are you paying attention to your reputation, value, marketability and relevance every day?

If you're like most people, you tend not to think about these attributes unless threatened, uncomfortable or unhappy.

Now comes the challenge: You may eschew self-promotion. You have been sponsored, recruited, managed through meritocracy and seduced by success indicators until the idea of "selling yourself" seems distasteful and humiliating. You've been effectively trained to believe that if you're a strong contributor, get along with others and behave loyally, you will be taken care of.

Would you run a business with this mindset?

Do you take your own career management as seriously as you take the management of your organization?

Your Pitch (Self-Promote with Panache)

"In the depth of winter, I finally learned that within me there lay an invincible summer."

— ALBERT CAMUS

Career progression as a Portable Executive is grounded in a well-honed ability to identify and articulate your most marketable attributes based on themes of satisfaction, achievement factors and results.

The tool below prepares you to understand how you can build on achievements and support portability from one work situation to the next, whether you shift career/life stage, geography or position. We call it "WOW":

Getting to WOW Instructions

Essential to portability is an updated record of your career highlights. You will use the information for: performance evaluation, career planning and management, analyzing your current against desired achievements, identifying areas of satisfaction, and projecting and advancing your next steps.

Creating a chart is very simple, and can be very useful if kept on your computer or PDA:

Your chart can have three columns headed:
- **Want** (need, situation or action)
- **Output** (what happened as a result)
- **Way** (how it was accomplished)

Every time you accomplish a goal, manage a project, solve a problem, create, innovate or initiate, note it on the tracking sheet.

Make note of those moments, interactions,

incidences and achievements that give you that sense of "WOW." As you keep track, a pattern will start to form of your highest achievements, commitment, competence, and results-oriented acknowledgement. Are you fulfilling your wants in particularly innovative ways? That's a true sign you're evolving into the Portable Executive.

Ideally, your WOW chart becomes a tracking sheet for use when you're evaluating your next career step, preparing for a performance review or interview or creating a resume or capabilities sheet for project/consulting work.

Cultivate Your Investors (Plan Your Exposure)

Every successful business has investors who provide necessary capital—and your career, as a business, is no different. Just as your typical organization depends on financial funding to keep running, your portable career runs on an different type of currency: information, introductions, leads and ideas.

Your "investors" are the people who can promote you, provide you with information and resources, connect you with beneficial people and contribute to your increased visibility. Connections and favors are more important than ever now that careers are self-managed and executives can no longer rely on the leadership succession, sponsorship and institutional talent management to take care of them.

Take a moment to consider your potential investors.

- What is important to them?
- How can they benefit from your talents?

Remember that, just as business investors expect a healthy monetary return, your own investors should be rewarded with reciprocity on your part. Keep track of what people have done for you, and don't hesitate to repay them with help, information, connections and leads. Portability requires exposure and ongoing self-marketing in a much more intentional, collaborative, creative and ego-free way than ever before.

Take Charge (Lead Your Experience)

Your transformation into a Portable Executive involves focus and strategy. The following chart, updated once per quarter, provides data by which you can measure your progress.

	Last Quarter	This Quarter	Next Quarter
Rate yourself on a quarterly basis using these measures.			
What measurable value have you added to your organization?			
Did your department or team play a primary role in your organization's profitability, productivity or improvement?			
Identify your three greatest professional strengths.			
Identify the areas of expertise you have contributed.			
Identify your three top professional development areas.			
What areas of expertise do you need to expand/develop?			
What are you doing to address these?			
What gets in your way?			
What relationships have you developed?			
Who do you need to get to know?			
Who needs to know you better?			
Identify your internal mentor(s). What are you doing to nurture these relationships?			
Measure your external visibility. What do you need to do to bolster this?			
What are your outside interests, hobbies or creative activities?			

LEAD PORTABLE TEAMS WITH PORTABLE PERSPECTIVE

To support your business strategy in times of change, you will be increasingly challenged to ensure your team's commitment and engagement during disruption. Here is where you can apply your Portable Executive mindset to build collective motivation.

Your team's workers may be distracted and disillusioned, still operating according to the precepts of the twentieth century workplace. If so, you can make a difference in their productivity and career potential.

You can drive their engagement and commitment by promoting the skills that will pay off for them in the flat, shrinking and competitive marketplace. One way you can do this is by establishing the "big rules" that formulate boundaries, ethics and etiquette in every encounter.

Motivators
First, examine and adjust your motivations and mindset as a leader:

- Are you focused on building loyalty?
- Do you believe your success as a leader rests on dedication and self-sacrifice in the interest of the company good?
- Do you expect and drive your team's adherence to these values and behaviors?

Then, identify your team's operating principles. Ask yourself and your team:

- Are you the Driver or the Driven?
- How do you get yourself to act?
- What is your underlying motivational tone?
- What do you want to create?

Intentions (Your Motivations Create)

DESIRE	OBLIGATION
Say: Want To, Wish To, Will Do, Can Do	Say: Try, Should, Must, Have To
Appreciate and Show Gratitude	Feel Resentment and Create Loyalty
Inspire	Engender Resistance
Aspire	Forced, Imposed Upon
Drawn to Goals	Dragged Down by Demands

- Desire energizes
- Obligation exhausts

Start regular career management dialogues with your team members. Have them analyze their own satisfaction factors, WOW elements and turn-ons. This will help liberate them from any security blanket/prison mindsets and prepare them for career accountability and self-promotion initiatives.

Change Championship

Now, instill both constructive momentum and change readiness in your team by becoming a change mentor.

First, assess your team's change readiness using the four-box model below. Observe team reactions to assignments, announcements, initiatives and shifts. Listen to the words your team members use and see where those words fall in the chart

CHANGE CHAMPIONSHIP

	EMBRACE	RESIST
ACT	Innovate Envision Expand Inspire Initiative Articulate (Ready to Change)	Flail No Focus Poor Prioritization Passive-Aggressive Subtly Undermine Complain (Cautious about Change)
HALT	Wait Watch Follow Question (Cautious about Change)	Shut Down Obstruct Hold Pattern Criticize (Resistant to Change)

Coach for Change

You will keep your team motivated and stimulated, whatever chaotic or disruptive situations may erupt, by helping them develop their own portable portfolios.

Impress upon them the three key elements of career effectiveness and mobility:

- Expertise
- Exposure
- Experience

And a continuous attitude of anticipating trends:
- Define and Diversify Your "Product" and "Trademark"
- Get Feedback (Market Analysis)
- Create a Marketing Plan
- Prepare and Follow a Quarterly Assessment, Review and Strategy Chart

These career management attitudes, skills and habits will enable your team members to create and self-market their portfolios for maximum benefit to their current (or future) organization. As they gain career confidence, your staff will be more change ready.

Portfolio Executive Career Conversations

"My employees have a one-day contract."
— JACK WELCH

In the Post-Millennium organization, loyalty and engagement can no longer be inspired by promises of promotions and job security. Your best bet is to help your team self-manage their careers. In laying out your mission, vision, values and strategy, challenge each of your members to self-promote in line with his or her career goals and strategy.

Teach them to:
- Set goals
- Inform you of achievements
- Pursue assignments of interest
- Volunteer for projects that develop new expertise
- Expand their visibility

Use the quarterly career plan as a jumping-off point for a dialogue with you

"Big Rules" Tip Sheet
- Follow the fairness doctrine: Make sure that everyone gets equally heard. Recognize cultural communication differences and mastery of the predominant language.

- Give information in advance so that everyone starts on an equal footing.

- Follow up and confirm accountabilities, agreements, expectations, time frames and next steps within 24 hours.

- Drive a "portability mindset" with regular (more often than annual) career discussions, including spot "coachable moments" that emphasize career self-knowledge, management and direction.

- Encourage staff members to stay with incentives

that build their reputation, increase their visibility and expand their expertise.

Share This With Your Team

Five Ways to Build a Portable Platform:

1. Run Your Career as You Do Your Business
- Be market aware and relevant
- Recognize, record, share and celebrate victories—especially small ones
- Invest in growth, development and innovation

2. Create a Portable Entity
- Stay visible and connected
- Track your strengths and build on them (using the WOW chart)
- Keep abreast of competitive data

3. Power Up
- Maximize constructive energy
- Mitigate obligation exhaustion

4. Create Happiness Around Yourself
- Instill "Big Rules"
- Recognition
- Reciprocity
- Relationship focus

CONCLUSION: THE PORTABLE EXECUTIVE ADVANTAGE

You now have the chance to become an innovative and influential leader. Opportunities will abound to expand, learn, develop and form beneficial short- and long-term connections. Each assignment or environment offers the chance to build experience, expertise and exposure. And if a particular position or company isn't the "right" fit, savvy, self-promoting executives have the option to seek out assignments that further enhance their career portfolio.

We invite you to join the ranks of these Portable Executives—Post-Millennium leaders with an adaptive mindset:

- You think of yourself as a free agent, a Post-Millennium leader who contributes and gains satisfaction and career continuity within organizations as an independent contributor and an entrepreneur.

- You view your current employer as your most important customer.

- Your work builds a portable portfolio, one in which you can invest, build and diversify based on value, market conditions and your own goals.

- You thrive as leaders of loyal and engaged teams.

- The people you lead understand the motivators of career satisfaction, as opposed to the seduction of career success.

- You have successful and satisfying careers, further leveraged by a habit of anticipating, adapting and offering your most marketable attributes to ever-changing marketplace needs.

- Your self-managed career plan replaces an

organizationally defined career path. You control your career via a focus on what matters most to your most important clients (your companies, customers and contacts).

- You self-promote rather than wait to be promoted or recruited.

- You freely dedicate your time and talents to current commitments that create value (and add to your portable portfolio of experience, exposure and expertise).

- You demonstrate your expertise and experience, and you keep your exposure at the top of your mind daily. You do this particularly when your work is great and your career is in a success and satisfaction mode.

You are change- and transition-ready!

PORTABILITY TIP SHEET

"I skate to where the puck is going to be, not where it has been."
— Wayne Gretzky

- Set expectations about stability and permanence.
- Remember that we are all always in transition in the Post-Millennium Workplace.
- Be fully committed to your current position/ organization. At the same time, consider your workplace contributions as additions to your portable portfolio.
- Build Career Satisfaction by your initiative and based on your criteria.
- Track your successes, satisfaction and the recognition you receive from your customers, company, colleagues and community.
- Expand your career management, thinking beyond organizational structures, career paths, promotions and succession plans.
- Create moves before you are disappointed, derailed or desperate.
- Accommodation and compromise are precursors for regret.
- Control your career with self-promotion rather than wait to be promoted.

Dr. Karen Otazo has been a global executive coach and mentor for executives in transnational companies worldwide for more than 25 years. Her second book, The Truth About Being a Leader *(2007), was recognized as one of the Top Five Best Business Books for 2007 by* Strategy and Business.

Dr. Otazo's experience makes her uniquely equipped to work with executives connecting cultures in global corporations, national subsidiaries, international ventures and strategic alliances.

She sits on the boards of Vital Voices Global Partnership, Citizens for Affordable Energy and Best Partners. Karen is a fellow of SoL, the Society for Organizational Learning, an international learning community dedicated to sustainable business.

www.global-leadership-network.com

Sheryl Spanier is a thought leader, media contributor and master practitioner of Executive Career Management who is sought out to coach and advise international leaders and their teams. After working as a consultant and market leader for four premier career management companies, she started her own firm in 2004. With more than 25 years in the field, Spanier combines empathy and pragmatism to coach clients in maximizing the interpersonal side of their business strategies and to lead individual and organizational change.

She is a member of Phi Beta Kappa, a founding member of the Association for Career Professionals International and is certified as a Fellow by the Institute for Career Certification International.

www.sherylspanier.com